Words of Comfort

EDITED BY PAUL S. McELROY

ILLUSTRATED BY VEE GUTHRIE

THE PETER PAUPER PRESS
Mount Vernon, New York

Be not afraid, neither be dismayed, for the Lord your God is with you wherever you may go!

WORDS OF COMFORT

The Hand of God

On the outskirts of the desert where village life goes along much as it did centuries ago, an eclipse of the moon occurred. As the shadow crept across the face of the moon, the residents were asked what was happening. Some replied that the moon was only sinking behind a mountain; others claimed it was merely the quarter phase of the moon; still others said it was hiding behind a cloud; but one old village sheikh, undisturbed by the growing darkness, imaginatively assured the onlookers that the phenomenon was the hand of God covering the moon. To be able to see the hand of God at work in the world is one of the greatest assets one can have. When the shadows are gathering for life's darker moments, the person who can still see God's hand at work, even in unfavorable circumstances, will be master of any situation life may impose upon him.

Suffering Is Not Punishment for Sin

In addition to physical pain, hardship, and mental anxiety, many people carry an additional burden of guilt because, like Job's accusers, they feel that suffering is inflicted as punishment for sin, which, knowingly or unwittingly, has been committed.

Whenever a person breaks a law, deliberately or inadvertently, somebody is hurt, damage is done, and a price must be paid. But there is consolation in the fact that suffering may be the consequence of wrong-doing rather than punishment for wrong-doing. Suffering is not imposed upon one by a jealous and revengeful God. A kind, benevolent God may allow His people to suffer, but this is quite different from assuming that God is sadistically imposing hardship.

Your Confidence and Hope

Is not your fear of God your confidence, and the integrity of your ways your hope?

JOB 4:6

Why Do the Righteous Suffer?

PROBABLY most of us feel justice demands that the wicked suffer and that the righteous be spared, but obviously the world does not operate on any such basis. The innocent suffer, at times, even more severely than the righteous. If perchance we suffer undeservedly, should we rail against God and allow ourselves to become embittered? Or, should we re-act, as Job did, and say that no purpose of God can be thwarted? Can we concede the supremacy of God, accept what life may impose upon us, and still stand firm in our love and loyalty to God?

Job and Jesus, as righteous men as ever lived, did not escape suffering, but on the contrary, suffered severely. In the way these righteous men endured suffering they demonstrated that one's attitude toward suffering can make one transcend the actual suffering itself.

The First Step

IN preparing for the unpredictable, the first step is to prepare for the predictable.

Rejoice in Suffering

WE rejoice in our sufferings, knowing that suffering produces endurance, and endurance produces character, and character produces hope, and hope does not disappoint us, because God's love has been poured into our hearts.

ROMANS 5:3-5

Content under All Circumstances

WITHIN each of us there are latent resources. St. Paul claimed that he had learned to be content in whatever circumstances he found himself. He knew what it was to have plenty and he knew what it was to live in deprivation. In any and in all circumstances, he learned the secret of facing abundance and want.

The Fruit of the Spirit

THE fruit of the Spirit is love, joy, peace, patience, kindness, goodness, faithfulness, gentleness, self-control; against such there is no law.

GALATIANS 5:22-23

A Blessing in Disguise

MISFORTUNE of any kind is pretty discouraging. It usually causes one to change his plans radically. A person can give in or give up. One may need, as a result, to seek a new vocation, but there is hope in the possibility that one may be more successful and more useful in the new vocation than he could have been in the old. Braille was trained as a cobbler, but an awl slipped and blinded him. As a result he developed the Braille system of reading for the blind.

It is also true that a handicap may make one more determined than ever to succeed and even excel. Glenn Cunningham, in spite of a serious burn on the leg, became the world's fastest miler.

There is consolation in the fact that what one regards as a misfortune may prove to be a blessing in disguise.

The Worth of Life

HELP me, O God, to learn from thee that the worth of life depends not upon the years of its duration, but on the spirit in which it is lived.

The Touch of God's Hand

Of course, there are untold things about death which perplex us. We wonder sometimes why God has not made it all more plain. The best answer to this may be that did we understand everything about death we might walk too much by sight and miss the touch of God's hand. Now we can put our hand into His that He may help us on our way.

Inner Strength

A young man, having just come through a difficult situation where he had been unjustly accused, but finally exonerated, remarked, "It is amazing what strength is added to a person when he knows he is right." Our strength is as the strength of ten, if only our heart is pure.

A Very Present Help

God is our refuge and strength, a very present help in time of trouble.

Psalm 46:1

Eternal Spring Is in the Heart

As death approached toward the end of a long life, Victor Hugo described his feelings in this way: "Winter is on my head, but eternal spring is in my heart. For half a century I have been writing my thoughts in prose, verse, history, philosophy, drama, romance, satire, tradition, ode, song. I have tried them all, but I feel that I have not said one thousandth part of what is in me. When I go down to the grave I can say, like many others, 'I have finished my day's work. But I cannot say, I have finished my life.' My day's work will begin again the next morning. The tomb is not a blind alley; it is a thoroughfare. It closes in the twilight to open in the dawn." Nothing is more certain than that we were created not to find the whole meaning of life here. Our destiny is beyond our mortal grasp.

Real Failure

THE only time a person really fails is when he blames his failure on somebody else.

Each Task Is Important

THERE are some who go through life performing routine tasks reasonably well, but without the feeling that there is any great importance attached to what they do or that it would make any difference if the work were never done. Only a relatively few individuals are driven by a deep conviction that what they are doing is important and that they have a distinctive mission to perform in doing it well. These few are the ones who change things for good or for evil, who largely determine the course which the world will take.

Such a sense of mission and urgency is greatly needed today. In the biblical story of Esther, it is said that her people were about to be destroyed because of the political maneuvering of a selfish individual. Mordecai, Esther's relative and foster-father, asked that she take personal risk and go uninvited to the King to plead for her people. In making this request, Mordecai said to Esther, "Who knows but you are come to the kingdom for just such a time as this?" There was great urgency in that plea, with the intention that perhaps the purpose of a whole life was tied up in that one moment.

Ideas operate by chain reaction, pass on from person to person, until great movements are started. Thus changes determine the destiny of man.

Within the Margins of Strength

IF we live under a handicap — and who of us does not live under a handicap of some kind — let us not pity ourselves. The tragedy is not to be found in the handicap, but rather in our inability to live within the margins of our strength. Even within our limitations there is an opportunity to improve ourselves and to find contentment. We should not be dissatisfied with what we have not, but rejoice with what we have, lest even that which we have be taken from us. The secret of rising above rather than being defeated by our handicaps, of being victors instead of victims of circumstance, is to be found not in rebellion but in adapting ourselves to circumstances and in making the most of situations that confront us.

Contributing Toward a Greater Goal

THERE is both joy and strength in being committed to something greater than yourself. If people would only let themselves be gripped by higher loyalties! Choose a cause that commands the best that is in you, one that taxes your imagination and resources to the full, one that is so fine and noble that you will give your life in pursuit of it, if necessary. Then you will not fail because a minor goal is not achieved, for you will have succeeded in helping to prepare the way for the achievement of a greater goal whose time has not yet come.

Do What You Can

I AM only one,
But still I am one.
I cannot do everything
But still I can do something;
And because I cannot do everything
Let me not refuse to do the something that
　　I can do.

EDWARD EVERETT HALE

Death Is a Friend

DEATH is not the enemy of life, but its friend, for it is the knowledge that our years are limited which makes them so precious. It is the truth that time is but lent to us which makes us, at our best, look upon our years as a trust handed into our temporary keeping.

Give Thanks in All Circumstances

ADMONISH the idle, encourage the fainthearted, help the weak, be patient with them all. Rejoice always, pray constantly, give thanks in all circumstances.

I THESSALONIANS 5:14-15

When Is Death Premature?

JIM ELLIOTT, a missionary, who was killed in South America, wrote in his youth, "We must not think it strange if God takes in youth those whom we would have kept on earth till they were older. God is peopling Eternity, and we must not restrict Him to old men and women."

Measuring Success

THE person who is spiritually worthy does not measure success in terms of whether his feeble strength and skill can triumph over the opposing forces. He measures success in terms of whether or not he does his part in what ought to be done. He believes that righteousness will ultimately triumph, and he willingly throws his own strength, such as it is, on the side of the morally right rather than on the side of expediency.

The truly religious person says in the face of danger and cruel opposition, "I may lose my life in the struggle that lies ahead, but I would rather lose my life fighting for a cause in which I believe than dying for a cause in which I do not believe."

Why Fear Death?

ALL men face what is inevitable. Why should death be feared? We begin to die as soon as we are born. At what moment, then, should we be most fearful of leaving the known for the unknown? Understandably, there may be a desire to postpone the transition — for ourselves and for our loved ones — but of what is there to be afraid?

Our physical body is lent to us as a house in which we live. When that dwelling becomes unfit for the purpose for which it was intended, a kind and benevolent nature has provided a way to get rid of that shell. That way is death.

Why then, should we be sad or rebellious? Death does bring changes and adjustments for those who are left behind. The warmth and association of former days are gone. The silence, the finality, the incommunicability disturb, but for our loved one who has triumphed, there should be rejoicing. Sorrow is centered on self.

BENJAMIN FRANKLIN

… Provided the Heart Is Right

WE shall steer safely through every storm,
    so long as our heart is right,
Our intention fervent, our courage steadfast,
    and our trust fixed on God.

ST. FRANCIS DE SALES

Suffering Can Be Redemptive

SUFFERING — whatever form it may take — seems negative, without purpose, and without value, but all suffering need not be so. Most of the time suffering is imposed upon us in ways beyond either our control or our understanding. Under such circumstances we pray for strength to endure and hope to profit in some way by the experience.

There are situations where individuals voluntarily choose suffering for themselves in order to protect another. Such actions are expressions of love, and love can transform suffering into sacrifice.

To do something for the sake of another, to suffer vicariously in behalf of another, is an expression of love, and love is redemptive!

Remote Results

You can never tell when you do an act
Just what the results will be;
But with every deed you are sowing a seed,
Though its harvest you may not see.

The Use of Time

It is the way we use our allotted time, whether it is seven or seventy years, that is important.

The Eternal Goodness

I LONG for household voices gone
For vanished smiles I long,
But God hath led my dear ones on
And He can do no wrong.

I know not what the future holds
Of marvel or surprise
Assured alone that life and death
His mercy underlies.

And so beside the silent sea
I wait the muffled oar;
No harm from Him can come to me
On ocean or on shore.

I know not where His islands lift
Their fronded palms in air;
I only know I cannot drift
Beyond His love and care.

JOHN GREENLEAF WHITTIER

Put No Obstacle in Another's Way

Let us "put no obstacles in any one's way, so that no fault may be found with our ministry, but as servants of God we commend ourselves in every way: through great endurance, in afflictions, hardships, calamities, beatings, imprisonments, tumults, labors, watching, hunger; by purity, knowledge, forbearance, kindness, the Holy Spirit, genuine love, truthful speech, and the power of God; with the weapons of righteousness for the right hand and for the left; in honor and dishonor, in ill repute and good repute."

II Corinthians 6:3-8

Religion and Suffering

It is the power to endure hardship, not a way to avoid it, that God gives. Escape from suffering is not promised to the religious. What religion does promise is victory over suffering, in the conviction that the moment's affliction weighs but little in the scale of everlasting values.

Love Has No Ending

GRIEF is a process which goes on night and day, and it takes time because the mind lets in only the amount of reality it can bear. It is deeply personal, for every man's grief is unique in its particulars. The only experience of life that is in any way comparable to grieving is that of being in love. Love consumes the lover, dominates his every moment. So it is with grief.

Although you cannot penetrate the mystery of life and death, you will be increasingly aware that you and your loved one came from God, you belong to God, and that you will go to God. Love is the most important thing in the world and love has no ending. At the time of death this loving part of us does not die but in some way continues with God.

A Matter of Viewpoint

I AM content with weaknesses, insults, hardships, persecutions, and calamities; for when I am weak, then I am strong.

II CORINTHIANS 12:10

Forgiveness for Failure

O GOD, forgive my readiness to accept short gains, my willingness to be content with less than the best, and my eagerness to do what I selfishly want to do. Make clean my heart within me, that I may not be tempted by that which diminishes me. If I must go where temptation is, give me the strength to withstand.

Bless the Lord

BLESS the Lord, O my soul; and all that is within me, bless His holy name!
Bless the Lord, O my soul, and forget not all His benefits!
Bless the Lord:

who forgives all your iniquities,
who heals all your diseases,
who redeems your life from destruction,
who crowns you with steadfast love and tender mercy,
who satisfies you with good things, so that your youth is renewed like the eagle's.

PSALM 103:1-5

Thank God for Work to Do

THANK God every morning when you get up that you have something to do which must be done, whether you like it or not. Being forced to work, and forced to do your best, will breed in you temperance, self-control, diligence, strength of will, content, and a hundred other virtues which the idle never know.

CHARLES KINGSLEY

Do Not Blame God

LET no man say when he is tempted, I am tempted of God: for God cannot be tempted with evil, neither tempteth he any man:

But every man is tempted when he is lured and enticed by his own desire.

JAMES 1:13-14

Reason for Failure

THE reason why people fail is that they do not pray. They try to do by themselves what no man can do unless God be with them.

The God of Comfort

BLESSED be . . . the Father of mercies and God
of all comfort, who comforts us in all our affliction, so that we may be able to comfort those
who are in affliction, with the comfort with
which we ourselves are comforted by God.

II CORINTHIANS 1:3-4

Do What You Can

WHEN the thing to which we devote our en-
ergies does not succeed, it does not necessarily
mean that we have failed. It is not our responsibility to set the whole world right, but it is our
responsibility to do what we can within our
little sphere of influence. That which we do
helps or hinders the progress of the world by
just so much.

Use What You Have

LET your desires be matched by your ability to
fulfill them. He is twice blessed who uses his
own gifts to capacity and does not envy the gifts
of others.

27

A Word for Our Time

In the seventeenth century when war had bitterly divided the people of Great Britain, there was built in Leicestershire the chapel of Staunton Harold. The dedication inscription is there today with its message of hope for our times:

IN THE YEAR 1653

WHEN ALL THINGS SACRED WERE

THROUGHOUT YE NATION

EITHER DEMOLISHED OR PROFANED

SIR ROBERT SHIRLEY, BARRONET,

FOUNDED THIS CHURCH:

WHOSE SINGULAR PRAISE IT IS

TO HAVE DONE THE BEST THINGS IN YE

WORST TIMES,

AND

HOPED THEM IN THE MOST CALLAMITOUS.

Whence Comes Our Help?

FROM whence does my help come?
My help comes from the Lord,
who made heaven and earth.

PSALM 121:1-2

Comfortable Living

KIRKEGAARD warns us of too comfortable living:
A wild duck settled in a cozy barn-yard where
he ate his fill for many months. He did not
spread his wings to fight the strong winds that
blew over his head. He stilled within him the
instinct to fly north or south with his brothers.
A year passed. One day he saw over his head
wild ducks in flight. His heart moved within
him, and he flapped his wings mightily as he
tried to rise from the ground. But the poor duck
had grown too fat. He could not rise. He is still
in the barn-yard.

So there are people whose hearts are moved,
their eyes light up, and they know where they
ought to be, but comfortable living has made
them too weak to respond and rise.

In Spite of Handicaps

WHY does not God grant to unusually gifted
people the advantage of good health? Why are
talented people often limited in the expression of
their gifts by physical handicaps and sickness?

The answer may be in the fact that sickness does not destroy one's talents; it may merely make it more difficult for one to execute his task. A handicap often sharpens one's powers and prompts one to do things he could not have achieved, if he had been well.

Beethoven was deaf; John Keats, Elizabeth Barrett Browning, Sidney Lanier, Chopin, Robert Louis Stevenson, and Thoreau were all tubercular; President Roosevelt was a victim of poliomyelitis. Yet illness was not allowed to hinder them. These people admittedly may have accomplished more with full health, but is it not also possible that their contributions could be made because of handicaps? Who knows but that their misfortunes gave them deeper insight and understanding?

A Parable

A TRAVELER in Switzerland asked a lad where the village of Kanderstag was. The reply was significant: "I do not know where Kanderstag is," said the lad, "but there is a road that leads to it."

Testing Produces Steadfastness

COUNT it all joy when you meet various trials, for you know that the testing of your faith produces steadfastness. And let your steadfastness have its full effect, that you may be perfect and complete, lacking in nothing.

JAMES 1:2

Be Thankful for Life

THANK God for life!
E'en though it bring much bitterness and strife,
And all our fairest hopes be wrecked and lost,
E'en though there be more ill than good in life,
We cling to life and reckon not the cost.
Thank God for life!

Do It Now

I EXPECT to pass through this world but once; any good thing, therefore, or any kindness that I can show to any fellow-creature, let me do it now; let me not defer it nor neglect it, for I shall not pass this way again.

Be Not Dismayed

HARDSHIP and disappointment, physical pain and mental suffering may come in life, but that does not mean that God is deserting us, nor does it mean that God is punishing us. God may love, yet not spare us from misfortune. The important thing is to know that no matter what happens God will care for us. "Be not afraid, neither be dismayed, for the Lord your God is with you where ever you may go."

Adversity Is Neither Fatal Nor Final

DISCOURAGEMENT, despair, disappointment, difficulty, defeat, disaster, death, failure, handicaps, hardships, misfortune, tribulations, trials, trouble; in brief, adversity, — from these there is no escape. No one can go through life without encountering some of these experiences. The tragedy is not that one is confronted with such circumstances, but that when they come they should, as Carlyle said, cause "the lamps of our soul to go out."

Adversity can make or break one. Many a

person has been ruined by adversity — and at times misfortune may demand serious adjustments, but that need not mean defeat. It is how one reacts to misfortune that counts. To accept what must be endured and to change what can be changed may bring comfort and consolation and a hope which can be the turning point between defeat and victory, between failure and success.

Help the Weak

WE who are strong ought to bear the infirmities of the weak.

ROMANS 15:1

When My Foot Slips

IF the Lord had not been my help, my soul would have dwelt in the land of silence.

When I thought, "My foot slips," thy steadfast love, O Lord, held me up.

When the cares of my heart are many, thy consolations cheer my soul.

PSALM 94:17-19

Detours May Be Opportunities

MANY a person has discovered that by bravely meeting difficult situations he has been pushed into accomplishing things which he never supposed he could do. Had Milton not been blind he probably would never have written much of his great poetry. John Bunyan's twelve tormenting years in Bedford jail afforded him the passion and the leisure to write *Pilgrim's Progress*. It was St. Augustine's sufferings that made possible his *Confessions*. Sickness and handicaps may mean that our careers will be thwarted in one way or another. Adversity may mean that we will witness our life's work reduced to ashes. Hardships may cause us to make detours, and detours are setbacks; but detours need not be defeats. They may prove to be opportunities!

Triumph Comes from Within

NOT in the clamor of the crowded street,
Not in the shouts and plaudits of the throng,
But in ourselves are triumph and defeat.

HENRY WADSWORTH LONGFELLOW

Religion Can Help

RELIGION can be of more help in time of trouble than we commonly suppose. Inherent in religion is the power to lift one to a point where one can carry on in spite of handicaps. Religion can give courage and hope. Religion can lend confidence and equanimity of spirit that will lift one out of the lowest depths. Religion is power.

To gain religious power one must strive to comprehend its truths. Its value cannot be gained suddenly in time of great need. Religion was a real power in the lives of our fathers, and we too often assumed that so long as it existed in their lives, a corresponding power, by virtue of inheritance, would be found in our lives. Little by little those fundamentals that are rooted in religion can be made a real part of our lives, so that in times of need we have sufficient inner strength to rise above our trials and tribulations.

The tragedy is not that affliction should come to us, but that when it comes there is not within us the power to withstand the winds of adversity that blow upon us.

Power to Win

THERE are the blind, O Lord, who have defied their infirmity; there are the helpless cripples in chairs and beds who will not suffer their affliction to break their spirits; there are those shut-ins who leap over their walls and minister to many. And we? Forgive us, that with health and liberty and some few powers to win, we are content to miss our chance to serve.

Let it Bless You

ADVERSITY and misfortune may handicap us in various ways, but there are many things we can do in spite of limitations. It is what we can do and not what we cannot that counts. In spite of setbacks there is still much that we can do. Many disabled people accomplish far more than do non-disadvantaged people. The secret of success lies in the will to do. The opportunity for achievement is still open to the less-privileged, provided they have sufficient determination to make the most of circumstances. The writer of the book of Genesis records the words which Jacob allegedly uttered when he wrestled with the "angel" at Peniel. Even though the struggle caused Jacob to limp throughout his life, he did not give up, but exclaimed with profound insight, "I will not let thee go until thou bless me." With Jacob, we can resolve not to let unfavorable experiences go until they bless us.

Making a Game of Difficulty

MAURICE RAVEL, afflicted by insomnia, fatigue, and occasional amnesia, was approached in 1929 to write a piano concerto for the one-armed pianist, Paul Wittgenstein. Ravel created the now famous *Concerto for the Left Hand Alone*. Ravel remarked to Wittgenstein regarding their handicaps, "I make a game of difficulty."

God Will Sustain You

CAST your burdens on the Lord, and He will sustain you.

PSALM 55:22

39

Misfortune Can Make or Break Us

MISFORTUNE can make or break us — depending upon how we take it. Adversity may be the very means of building a richer, fuller life than we have ever known before. Suffering accepted may place us in a more advanced position in our career and give us a serenity which may well prove our most rewarding experience. Think not upon what may be lost through adversity, but let the mind dwell upon the abundance that remains.

How We Play the Game

IT matters little whether we win or lose; it is how we play the game that counts.

In Time of Distress

IN my distress I called upon the Lord;
to my God, I cried for help.
From His temple He heard my voice
and my cry to Him reached His ears.

PSALM 18:6

Power to Overcome

WE may have the wish to be masters of ourselves in the face of adversity, but it is quite another thing to possess the power which will make us masters of our fate. The power is there if we will but cultivate and nurture it. Just as man can, over a period of years, gain enough knowledge — which is a form of power — to build a bridge which is safe for traffic and thereby enable him to overcome the river, the obstacle to his progress, so can we, over a period of time, gain enough faith — which is the power within us — to enable us to stand anything that can happen to us in adversity.

Mourn Not for Me

MOURN not for me, for frailty is left behind. I face the next step in life's pilgrimage with the great calm with which God has so richly blessed me, knowing we are His children whether we live or die, and that our deep love which endureth all things is everlasting.

ELSIE BUSH WOOLSEY

Blessings in Adversity

ON first thought it may seem an inconsistency to expect blessings from adversity, but there is evidence that the blessings of adversity may be more fruitful than the benefits of prosperity.

Adversity has shown that it is better to seek strength from within than to rely upon forces from without.

Adversity has also shown that the worthwhile things of life are spiritual qualities rather than material substances. The things which are seen are temporal and pass away, but the unseen, spiritual things, are real and eternal.

Adversity can teach a sense of values, — that it is more blessed to give than to receive, that it is more edifying to share than to hoard.

Afflicted But Not Crushed

WE are afflicted in every way, but not crushed; perplexed, but not driven to despair; persecuted, but not forsaken; struck down, but not destroyed.

II CORINTHIANS 4:8-9

Tapping Your Reserves

THERE is greater power within you than you know. Your doubts and fears are often caused by your lack of confidence. In emergency you have discovered that you can run faster, show more courage, suffer longer, and work harder than you normally can. If you live on the surface of your power, never tapping your reserves, you will never discover how much you really can do. If you know that you and God are working together, there is no limit to what you may do. With such faith you can move mountains. Alone you can go only so far, but with God all things are possible. When you let God enter in you and work through you, then there is a power that is infinite.

Our Heritage from the Past

EVERY generation enjoys the use of a vast hoard bequeathed to it by antiquity, and transmits that hoard, augmented by fresh acquisitions to future ages.

THOMAS MACAULAY

If You Cannot Excel

IF you constantly compare yourself with others, you may become unhappy or boastfully proud, for there will always be people greater or lesser than you. Your friends may excel in one thing and it is impossible for you to excel in all that your friends do. Remember your mediocre gifts may contribute more toward the success of some project than the extraordinary talents of some one else. Take consolation in the worthiness of what you can do and be content in doing the best you can!

A Lesson from History

CHARLES A. BEARD is credited with making these observations from history:

When it gets darkest, the stars come out.
When a bee steals from a flower, it also fertilizes that flower.
Whom the gods would destroy, they first make mad.
The mills of the gods grind slowly, but they grind exceedingly fine.

The Beginning or the End?

THERE is as much reason to assume that death is the beginning of a glorious adventure as to assume that it is the end of all. Surely, if a milligram of musk will give out perfume for seven thousand years, and a milligram of radium give out light for seventy thousand years, then the human soul, which is far more precious than musk or radium, will live for more than seventy years.

The Dawn Has Come

DEATH is not extinguishing the light, but putting out the lamp because the dawn has come.

RABINDRANATH TAGORE

Virtue in Endurance

BLESSED is the man who endures trial, for when he has stood the test, he will receive the crown of life which God has promised to those who love Him.

JAMES 1:12

On Living under Pressure

WHAT is the secret of living under tension and pressure? How can you remain serene and effective, even though problems crowd in upon you? Someone said, "All the water in the sea cannot sink a ship unless the water gets inside." All the troubles in the world cannot sink a man unless they invade his inner life. It is possible, as a Roman emperor once said, "to retire into yourself. There is no retreat more peaceful, less troubled, than the one you find within your own soul." May God help you to find the peace which passes all understanding.

Our Loved Ones Are Near

TEACH us to believe that our loved ones are no farther away than Thou art, and Thou art very near. Amen.

Failures Contribute to Success

MAN can be a failure many times and still succeed.

The Longer We Live

THE longer we live the stronger those ties become which attract us toward another world, and the fewer and weaker are those that attach us to this.

The Real Self

A FRIEND who was crippled by infantile paralysis and lived for over seventy years as a semi-invalid once wrote:

"I wish so much that people could be made to consider their bodies in what, it seems to me, is the proper relation to their *real selves*. I refuse to believe that my body is *myself*. It is only the house I live in, and anything that happens to *me*. If our material house is damaged by wind, fire, or just ravages of time, we are made uncomfortable, as we have to live in it, and so we like to keep it in as good a state of repair as possible.

"That line of thought has been a great comfort to me also in regard to death. I absolutely believe that when that event takes place still nothing has happened to the *real person* I knew and loved. He or she has just slipped out of that 'house' leaving it looking just as it did, but empty as any physical house is when the occupants have moved. And how different an empty house seems! We walk through rooms which may look the same with furniture unchanged, etc., and yet we feel so different, for it all seems so empty, but really only lacking the personality which for us gave it life."

To the Unseen Shore

SOMETIME at eve when the tide is low
I shall slip my moorings and sail away;
With no response to the friendly hail
Of kindred craft in the busy bay.
In the silent hush of the twilight pale,
When the night stoops down to embrace the
    day,
And the voices call in the water's flow, —
I shall slip my moorings and sail away.

Through the purpling shadows that darkly trail
O'er the ebbing tide of the Unknown Sea,

I shall fare me away, with a dip of sail
And a ripple of waters to tell the tale
Of a lonely voyager sailing away
To the mystic isles where at anchor lay
The crafts of those who have sailed before
O'er the Unknown Sea to the Unseen Shore.

A few who have watched me sail away
Will miss my craft from the busy bay;
Some friendly barks that were anchored near,
Some loving souls that my heart held dear,
In silent sorrow will drop a tear, —
But I shall have peacefully furled my sail
In moorings sheltered from storm and gale,
And greeted the friends who have sailed before
O'er the Unknown Sea to the Unseen Shore.

LIZZIE CLARK HARDY

A Comrade Rides Ahead

TIME brings us change and leaves us fretting;
    We weep when ev'ry comrade goes —
Perhaps too much, perhaps forgetting
    That over yonder there are those
    To whom he comes and whom he knows.

50

I would not hold our loss too lightly;
 God knows, and we, how deep the pain;
But, friends, I see still shining brightly
 The brightest link in all our chain
 That links us to a new domain.

For this I swear, because believing,
 Time breaks no circle such as this.
However hurt, however grieving
 However much a friend we miss,
 Between the worlds is no abyss.

For friendship binds the worlds together —
 World over there, world over here.
From earth to heaven is the ether
 That brings the earth and heaven near
 And makes them both a bit more dear.

Not weaker now our chain, but stronger;
 In all our loss and all our ill
We shall now look a little longer
 At every star above the hill
 And think of him, and have him still.

Whatever vales we yet may wander
 What sorrows come, what tempests blow,
We have a friend, a friend out yonder

To greet us when we have to go —
Out yonder someone that we know.

To all eternity he binds us;
He links this planet with the stars;
He rides ahead, the trail he finds us,
And where he is and where we are
Will never seem again so far.

Douglas Malloch

God at Work in Adversity

Nydia, the blind flower girl in Bulwer Lytton's *The Last Days of Pompeii*, a sad and pitiful figure, moves through the story, groping her way unerringly about the winding streets of Pompeii. When Vesuvius buries the city in molten lava, all is in total darkness and terror-stricken inhabitants rush frantically to and fro in an effort to escape. They are lost in the awful blackness. But Nydia, accumstomed as she is to the dark, goes swiftly through the streets and rescues the one she loves. If only we could know for what our crosses may be fitting us! God may be at work in us in times of darkness.

On the Death of a Loved One

WE may reason bravely that our loved one has lived to a ripe old age and we may be relieved to know that his suffering is over at last. We admit philosophically that death has come as a blessing, but no matter what our attitude may be, it hurts to lose a loved one. Whether death has come after prolonged illness in old age, or suddenly in the prime of life, we must nevertheless be grateful for the years we have been privileged to be together, and for the joys and sorrows that the relationship has afforded.

A Greater Plan

THERE is a plan far greater than the plan we
know,
There is a landscape broader than the one we
see.
There is a heaven where storm-tossed souls
may go —
Some call it death — some immortality.

Some call it death — this seeming endless sleep.
I call it birth — the soul at last set free.

'Tis hampered not by time nor space — yea
weep —
Why weep at death? 'Tis immortality.

Farewell, dear voyager — 'twill not be long.
Thy work is done — now may peace rest
with thee.
Thy kindly thought and deeds — they will
live on.
This is not death — 'tis immortality.

Farewell, dear voyager — the river winds and
turns,
The cadence of thy song wafts near to me.
And now thou knowest the thing that all men
learn,
There is no death — there's immortality.

Not Neglected

WE ought to be of good cheer in the face of
death and to hold firmly that this one thing, at
least, is true: no evil can come to a righteous
man either in life or in death, and his interests
are not neglected by the gods.

SOCRATES

A Benevolent Act of God

WITH our finite minds we cannot understand the mysteries of life or of death, and not understanding, we are impatient with what for the moment seems inimical to us. Yet in our sober moments we know that death is a kind and benevolent act of God.

Cloudy Days Are Needed

ALL sunny skies would be too bright,
All morning hours mean too much light,
All laughing days too gay a strain;
There must be clouds, and night, and rain,
And shut-in days, to make us see
The beauty of life's tapestry.

I Salute You

I AM your friend, and my love for you goes deep. There is nothing I can give you which you have not; but there is much, very much that, while I cannot give it, you can take. No Heaven can come to us unless our hearts find rest in it today.

Take Heaven! No peace lies in the future which is not hidden in this present little instant. Take Peace!

The gloom of the world is but a shadow. Behind it yet within our reach is — Joy. There is radiance and glory in darkness, could we but see, and to see, we have only to look. I beseech you to look....

Life is so generous a giver, but we, judging its gifts by their covering, cast them away as ugly or heavy or hard. Remove the covering and you will find beneath it a living splendour, woven of Love, by Wisdom and Power. Welcome it, grasp it, and you touch the Angel's hand that brings it to you. Everything we call a trial, a sorrow, or a duty, believe me that Angel's hand is there, the Gift is there, and the wonder of an overshadowing presence. Our joys, too, be not content with them as joys. They, too, conceal diviner Gifts.

Life is so full of meaning and purpose, so full of beauty beneath its covering — that you will find earth but cloaks your heaven. Courage then to claim it, that is all! But courage you have, and the knowledge that we are pilgrims together, wending through unknown country . . . home!

And so, at this time, I greet you, not quite as the world sends greetings but with profound esteem, and with the prayer that for you, now and forever, the day breaks and shadows flee away.   FRA GIOVANNI — 1513.

One View of Death

IT may be of help to know how some people have viewed the inevitable. Near the end of a long life, Lyman Abbott, expressed it this way: — "I have fought a good fight, I have often faltered, but I have kept up the race. I have been besieged all my life with doubts, but I have kept my faith. I look forward to the great adventure with awe, but not with apprehension. I have enjoyed my work, my home, my friends, my life — I shall be sorry to part with them. But always I have stood in the bow looking forward with hopeful anticipation to the life before me. When the time comes for my embarkation and I put out to sea, I think I shall still be standing in the bow looking forward with eager curiosity

and glad hopefulness to the new world to which
the unknown voyage will bring me."

God Does Care

WHEN the righteous cry for help, the Lord
   hears, and delivers them out of all their
   troubles.
The Lord is near to the broken-hearted
   and saves the crushed in spirit.
Many are the afflictions of the righteous;
   but the Lord delivers him out of them all.
PSALM 34:17-19

Saint Teresa's Book-mark

      LET nothing disturb thee,
      Nothing affright thee;
      All things are passing;
      God never changeth;
      Patient endurance
      Attaineth to all things;
      Who God possesseth
      In Nothing is wanting;
      Alone God sufficeth.

Gone Where?

IMAGINE you are standing on the seashore. A ship at your side spreads her white sails to the morning breeze and starts for the blue ocean. She is an object of beauty and strength and you stand and watch her until at length she hangs like a speck of white cloud just where the sea and sky meet and mingle with each other: "There, she is gone."

Gone where? Gone from your sight, that is all. She is just as large in hull and mast and spar as when she left your side and just as able to bear her load of living freight to the place of her destination. Her diminished size is in you, not in her.

And just at the moment when someone at your side says, "She's gone," there are other eyes watching for her coming and other voices ready to take up the glad shout, "Here she comes!" And this is what we call dying — this is life!